W9-BGS-818

# AE'S LETTERS TO MÍNANLÁBAIN

THE MACMILLAN COMPANY
NEW YORK · BOSTON · CHICAGO · DALLAS
ATLANTA · SAN FRANCISCO

MACMILLAN & CO., LIMITED
LONDON · BOMBAY · CALCUTTA
MELBOURNE

THE MACMILLAN COMPANY
OF CANADA, LIMITED
TORONTO

# AE'S LETTERS
# TO MÍNANLÁBÁIN

With an Introduction

By

LUCY KINGSLEY PORTER

NEW YORK

THE MACMILLAN COMPANY

1937

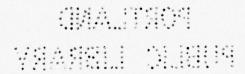

## Foreword

This handful of letters was written to my husband and me between 1930 and 1935. My husband's side of the correspondence is missing as AE destroyed all letters written to him, except those received during his last illness.

I have made the fewest possible changes in the manuscript, correcting spelling and punctuation only when necessary. The slight omissions have been indicated and the dates given in brackets have been supplied by me. But the quotations in the text of the letters I have left untouched—precisely as AE spontaneously recalled them.

LUCY KINGSLEY PORTER

Elmwood
November 1936

The frontispiece of AE is reproduced through the courtesy of the photographer and owner of the copyright, Zlata Coomaraswamy.

# AE'S LETTERS TO MÍNANLÁBÁIN

"What other people don't want I usually find has value for me." This was the answer Kingsley Porter, my husband, gave when I asked why he had rented Marble Hill, a manor house in Ireland he had never seen and which was far away from the high crosses and the other archaeological interests that country held for him. We both laughed, for we knew that the Americans who had leased this Irish place for two summers (also without seeing it) would prefer to lose the rent rather than return for the second season. We sub-let it from them, little guessing how significant the gifts of Donegal—AE and the sea—were to Kingsley. These letters show the relationship that grew up between the two men which started and ended within the sound of that encompassing sea.

For about thirty summers AE had been in the habit of going to this part of Ireland. When I asked him once why he didn't try the continent for a change he said he wanted to know Donegal first. He used to stay with Janie-on-the-Hill at Ballymore, in a cottage belonging to farmer folk, whose simplicity and genuineness were as characteristic of AE as of them. Here he had as neighbors his friend and her family, Lota Law, who was born at Marble Hill and still owns that estate. When fog and rain shut out the near-by sea the view was like a flowering bush without its blossoms. But let the sun shine and the sea dance and all was fragrance and glistening silver petals. Between great headlands the ocean enters Sheephaven Bay, winding its way among green peninsulas and little land-locked islands before it rolls over a mile of golden sands. How often AE has painted children playing upon this strand! It seemed indelibly engraved upon his mind, so that he repeated it unconsciously in verse and on canvas. The mountains of Lough Swilly (the Lake of the Shadows) in the far distance step from the sea into the sky.

When Kingsley and I walked inland over the high boglands we sometimes kicked up a dust of golden bees from the purple heather. This always meant bright sunshine so that even with a casual glance we could plainly distinguish four dots on the open Atlantic—the Tory archipelago. These islands came to float in Kingsley's mind as naturally as in the sea. He was not content until we had made trips of exploration to them. Yet they still hovered in his memory. The more he knew them, the more they possessed him.

AE's thought did not seem to go out over the ocean. At farthest, it would wade from the shore. This may have been due to his short-sightedness, while Kingsley's St. John-eagle-like vision led him always to focus his interest upon some distant point.

The first evening AE came to dine with us at Marble Hill Kingsley walked home with him after dinner. It was towards morning before he returned. "Never have I heard such beautiful talk," he said to me, "and never have I had

2

a harder time to find the way." With only the stars as lantern, taking down and putting back rails in fences, all but wading through streams and being brought up short by unexpected peat-hags, would have appalled many men of younger years than AE.

Although their walks by night were continued, AE did not come to dine with us again. He found it stuffy indoors and a tedious waste of time. So he came instead to afternoon tea, staying on to talk to us on the terrace. Our guests were too much engrossed to notice the passing of time. When dinner was announced we invited him in. He would not come, neither would he stop talking. As there was no end to a paragraph I could not break in. The soup got cold on the table. The household became restive. They made violent signs behind his back for me to stop him. But AE, all unconscious, talked on. At this point Kingsley saved the situation and the dinner by sauntering off with AE, who still under full steam continued his conversation.

The spell of Donegal fell more and more upon Kingsley, AE's cast of mind not the least factor in the charm. One evening on the spur of the moment we went to the Laws' near-by cottage overhanging the sea to sign the lease for Marble Hill for the following summer. By training cautious and conservative in all his business transactions, Kingsley said to me, in the nature of an apology as we walked home, "You see, I knew everyone would want to come to Donegal next summer so I thought it best to act quickly."

Only a few weeks later he saw for the first time Glenveagh Castle on Lough Veagh, an estate about fifteen miles

3

inland. It was a little kingdom of high mountains, wild moorlands, lakes and streams, and the nearest post-office, seven miles away, was Mínanlábáin. To Kingsley it was Suibhne Geilt's ever-delightful Glen Bolcain—

> *"Water of bright Glen Bolcain*
> *listening to its many birds;*
> *its melodious, rushing streams*
> *its islands and its rivers. . . .*
> *If I were to wander alone*
> *the mountains of the brown world,*
> *better would I deem the site of a single hut*
> *in the Glen of mighty Bolcain. . . .*
> *Its sheltering holly and its hazels . . .*
> *the bellowing of its stags . . .*
> *its pure water without prohibition*
> *'tis not I that hated it."*

This estate held another fascination for Kingsley. In the gentler part of the landscape, at Gartan, Columcille—the most Irish of all Irish saints—is traditionally believed to have been born. A small mound and large flat stone mark the site where peasants on their Columcille pilgrimage come to pray. One often sees the kneeling figures while curlews, plaintively calling, circle above them through the evening sky.

This demesne which for over twenty years had been sleeping in neglect awaiting a purchaser suddenly found one in Kingsley. He must buy it at once—Marble Hill could

4

be disposed of for a season. For here his search ended—at last he had found wilderness of beauty and holy solitude.

There was only one lack—the sea. But that could be arranged! Kingsley had a little cottage—like the fishermen's—built for us on Inish Bofin, the smaller of the two inhabited islands in the group of four that lie out in the ocean north of Donegal. Although the nearest of the islands—it is only three miles from the shore as against Tory's nine—it is more remote from civilization. Unlike Tory, it has no government launch to deliver mail three times a week—weather permitting. Neither has it church nor store.

New as our stone hut was, it seemed to have taken root and to be growing out of the island soil. The song Suibhne sang of his little oratory in Tuaim Inbir, which Kingsley knew in an eighth century version, seemed to him to describe our island refuge—

*". . . God from heaven*
*He is the thatcher who hath thatched it.*

*A house wherein wet rain pours not*
*a place wherein thou fearest not spear-points,*
*bright as though in a garden*
*and it without a fence around it."*

Beyond, out towards the north, cliffs like fingers narrowly opened, stretch into the wide Atlantic. This more forbidding part of the island, where our little house stands, is connected only by a narrow bridge of sands with the flat more friendly part where the fishermen live. Like clothes

5

hung out to dry their white houses in a long line are built as near as they can get them to the mainland. When, snug in our little hut at night, listening to "the voice of the white seas," we wondered if the strip of sand connecting like a thread the two halves of the island might not break and the morning find us adrift on the fifth island of the Tory archipelago.

Not one of these island people would have spent a night in our cottage. It was "too lonesome," too much a part of the open sea they had so many reasons to dread.

One of the two fishermen who took charge of us—the one who lived on the island—was Pat Coll, young, handsome and strong. Once he had floated eight or nine hours in mid-ocean, clinging to a spar of the wrecked salmon boat. (Caught in a sudden fog, a steamer had cut the long row-boat in two.) Pat had watched first his old uncle, then his two cousins—all Colls—drown one by one as they had to let go their piece of wreckage. At day-break a little steamer rescued him. Thus at Inish Bofin one name had been erased from the long list of those lost at sea.

Our other fisherman, Owen McGee, lived on the mainland, and took care of our row-boat, and sailed her with us. He was a native of Inish Bofin, but as Mrs. McGee was not, he could not live on the island—no shore woman would. She was a pretty youngish woman and as devoted to us as either of the men. Whenever we had to launch the boat at low tide at Magheraroarty, the place on that coast nearest to Inish Bofin, she was there ready to give a hand, walking right into the icy water—if it were winter or early spring—with her shoes and stockings on, wetting her long skirts up

6

to her knees. When we remonstrated, she would say laughingly in the midst of her strenuous pushing, "Ach! sure, it's good for me corns." She was one of the few women of her age on that shore who knew English. At other times, when we went to the island alone in our fragile curragh, she was anxious and would call after us, "May the Blessed Virgin bring you safely back to land." To her, islands were only another form of the Protean sea.

Once when a storm of several days' duration seemed, to us at the castle, at last to have subsided sufficiently to risk our going to the island, we motored hopefully to Magheraroarty, but were greeted by sad, silent faces.

One of the island girls, marooned on the mainland by the storm, came up to us and said soberly, "You can't get over. I've been here meself these four days and can't get back. A ninth wave would surely catch you and swamp the boat." Perplexed by her sadness we asked if anything were wrong. "Biddie Coll's dead," she said laconically. "It was three nights ago. The rain heavy, the sea fierce, and the wind high, but we could see the flames of the bonfire on the island so we knew some one lay dead. It was on the hill but not in back of the first house so my folks was safe. Owen, beside me as we watched, thought it was his old father but we could kinder count and the eighth house was safe. Then we all saw plainly—it was the Coll's—the last house. So we knew Biddie's baby had come too soon. They couldn't fetch no doctor. They couldn't launch no boat. One or both is dead and who knows when they can bring 'em over to the church-yard? And me not there when they waked her."

7

A fortnight passed before we again visited Inish Bofin. We found the bed-ridden grandmother, whom Pat's sister, Biddie Coll, had come home from America to nurse, up by the turf fire, always burning in their snug little cottage, which Biddie had kept so beautifully clean and neat. The old woman was jerking back and forth an orange-crate which served as a cradle for the motherless unkempt baby. The poor little thing was coughing. It had taken cold going over to the mainland for the christening. An extremely long, narrow, complicated-looking rubber tube had a nipple on one end while the other rested in a pitcher with a little milk in it. This was the way the baby was fed. The cows were going dry on the island but so long as there was a drop of milk it would be saved for Biddie's child. Somehow the baby did pull through the winter and survive—nourished perhaps by the love of the entire island community.

We took AE with us once for a day's trip to Inish Bofin. He did not greatly enjoy it, nor was he interested in the individual islanders. His mind was too used to dwell on "things invisible to mortal sight" to differentiate people who had no intimate connection with his own life nor with his inner thought.

It was in the winter of 1931, in America, that AE first came to us as a house-guest, when he was giving lectures in or near Boston. What stands out most distinctly to me during his stay at Elmwood—our home in Cambridge—is his conscientiousness about his lectures. If a car were to call for him he was ready with overcoat on, hat in hand sitting in the hall fully twenty minutes before the appointed hour. Money which meant so little to him in itself when given in exchange for his own lectures assumed a real importance. In fact he had been willing to come to America to give these lectures in order to be able to care for his wife, who was now in ill health. If Kingsley happened to pass, he eagerly began a conversation, his eloquence arrested only by the arrival of the automobile.

One Sunday afternoon we invited many people to meet him. I have since wondered if they might not more truthfully say they had met him than if they had been introduced and shaken his hand as they passed by in line. I arranged to have him sit surrounded by a small circle of people. Conversation was started. I am sure he was quite unconscious that from time to time two or three of the group would noiselessly give up their places to others until all had sat at his feet. It was like the fence in front of Elmwood. Since the eighteenth century picket by picket it has been restored and yet is always the same Colonial fence.

AE's first visit to us in Ireland was the following summer, in July, 1931. With some trepidation we asked him to leave the sweetness and simplicity of Janie-on-the-Hill, to come to be our guest at Glenveagh Castle.

We went to fetch him in the motor. A white road flung across the heather-grown mountains drops precipitously in four miles from the lodge-gate to the court-yard of the castle. That day the sky was stretched very tight for the rolling and unrolling of the masses of clouds whose shadows raced with them over the treeless land and over the lakes. Distant mountains rounded or flat appeared to disappear on the horizon, heightening the grandeur, punctuating the loneliness. AE turned back to us from the front seat, where he liked best to ride, saying that we were passing through a part of the world as ancient as time itself, the poet accurately sensing the geological formation. A sharp turn and the castle suddenly was before us. Equally suddenly the heather, bog-cotton and bracken of the moors ceased as if commanded to go no farther that an exotic vegetation might stripe, like an oasis, the wasteland of the mountain. The castle, proud of the conquest, lifted its head like a gigantic lily high above the "incense-bearing trees" and the taller pines.

When we showed AE his quarters he asked humorously, "But where can I throw matches on the floor and not have them picked up?" So an empty oval room was allotted him for this purpose and for his canvases. Missing guests were sure to be found there, sitting on boxes, puffing their pipes and dexterously dropping matches on the stone pavement to the rhythm of AE's sonorous sentences.

At Janie's, afternoon tea was his evening meal, which gave him the hours when day reluctantly and slowly was being conquered by night to wander under the ever-changing sky. With us, he, the lightest and most indifferent of eaters, was forced, at the enchanting hour of eight, to sit with his legs under a dinner table. Graciously he complied, prompted by his sense of punctiliousness toward his hosts. He was rewarded by the eager audience which he acquired, for with him the service between brain and lips was flaw-less.

Anyone who has ever listened to AE, in reading many of these letters will hear the musical cadences that rising and falling lead to the vocal climax—always a perfect-fitting garment to the thought. At this point his eyes would open wide behind his spectacles and you could see they were a deep violet blue. His youthful complexion would assume the lines of smile or laughter—the only wrinkles on his bearded, kindly face. He enjoyed his own impishness as much as anyone. Sometimes his fat stubby hands—which looked as if they would be useless except where pen and brush were concerned, but were, however, surprisingly adroit, were it not a matter of cups and saucers!—would be used in gesticulation, or his shoulders lifted in emphasis. But if ever words needed no external aid they were AE's.

His mind at sixty odd remained immune from the mod-ern pastime of forgetting names. He used to say he owed his memory to poverty. Having so few books in youth he unconsciously memorized whatever he read. This ability tended to set his conversation into subjects. The type once laid down, ever afterwards the words (which fortunately were always the right ones) kept their same positions. But his repertoire was so great and the moment itself created always so much new talk he seldom repeated these fixed topics unless you asked him to tell again a certain experi-ence or a certain story. In these letters, however, there is always spontaneity, due perhaps to the haste in which they were written—as if he were eager to be through with them to have more time for the spoken word.

The evenings at Glenveagh would find everyone gathered about AE before the open turf fire in the library. This room, high in the tower, was swung over the lake into the sunset which lingered into the night tinging to gold the orange of Biddie O'Donnell's home-spun curtains. "A bit of the setting sun, they'll be, sir," she had said, curtseying to Kingsley, when we had motored over to the weavers at Dunlewy and had asked her to make them for us, for this new home of ours here in Ireland, "and sure I'll be honored, sir, to have my work hanging at the windows of the castle."

There was no question of reading aloud when AE was there to think aloud to us. Nor did we need to refer to books. Almost any poem in English that was spoken of AE could recite. I can see him now turning toward me with surprise, almost offence, when at about one in the morning I suggested breaking up and going to bed. Kingsley's Greek sense of hospitality was equally offended by my dashing cold water on conversation still in flame. Laughingly AE would brush it away, stand up, light his candle and look on the library shelves to find a book as a night-cap.

He was not so much interested in the old annals of Ireland or the translations of the Irish Text Society; his intimacy was more with the Druidic gods of ancient Ireland and with Finn and Cuchulain, who had come to him through the romantic channels of O'Grady and Lady Gregory. Nor did Kingsley's rare old guides and histories of Ireland—especially of Donegal—interest him. But our *Arabian Nights*—the English translation of Mardus' French translation—did. We waited next morning to have him tell us of some tale of mysticism or recite some Persian poem he had found there. One rainy morning he brought to the breakfast table the following rhyme he had scribbled off on his way down stairs.

*Kingsley Porter's ideal poem*
*imagined by AE.*

*Here's where joy may be found*
*When lanes are all in flood*
*And my ecstatic boots*
*Are tramping through the mud.*

*Be kind, wind, to Glenveagh!*
*Never forget to blow*
*Vast leagues of watery mist*
*To set my heart a-glow!*

*O rain, O lovely rain,*
*That keeps me always wet*
*Through coat and shirt—to skin,*
*You are my pet, my pet!*

$$\frac{\begin{array}{r}19\\7\end{array}}{31}$$

He seemed to need as little sleep as he did food. Always he was out-of-doors in the morning before anyone else was out of bed. When I told him that my snobbish, English-trained Irish parlor-maid wondered if he would mind leaving his one suit of clothes in his dressing-room so she could press it while he slept, adding apologetically, "I know, Madam, Mr. Russell, like Mr. Porter and Father Gallagher, don't think of things of this world," he chuckled and asked me to tell Holmes how James Stephens had described him in the *Char-Woman's Daughter*, "There was a tall man with a sweeping brown beard whose heavy overcoat looked as though it had been put on with a shovel." He made the accompanying drawing as his signature in our guest-book after this visit. Another year he wrote, "Caught three poems and one fish. 'Good hunting'." The poems were: *Incarnation*, *Distraction*, and *Lost Talisman*. They came as much of a surprise to him as the fish, which had been hooked while he held for a moment the rod of a fisherman beside him in the boat.

Perhaps the greatest interest in these letters lies in being able to follow the process of the creating of his new book, *The Avatars*, which proved to be his last work in prose. In the letter of Friday, which I date August 7, '31, he says, "I have started on my next book, roughly written four chapters and in a vague way see its ultimate shape and dominating mood." The subsequent letters explain why the book was not finished as he hoped, "by the end of the year [1931] or thereabouts," and why it dragged along so many months more. It was not until July 8, 1933, the date fixed upon for AE's visit to Kingsley and me at Glenveagh, that he brought with him an advance copy of *The Avatars*. Eagerly he had been anticipating Kingsley's pleasure in the book. But that day was to find AE and me alone and was to pierce my spirit with the deepest pain I was ever to know.

I remember the day of his arrival in Donegal. It was night and I was sitting, tiller in hand, in the stern of Kingsley's blue row-boat as she rode the waves of the Atlantic, on my last voyage from Inish Bofin to the mainland—Owen and I alone in the boat. I was too stunned not to be calm as I steered her to the shore. "The Swan" was written in Gaelic on her bow—an unlucky name the fishermen had told us. It was still light. The thunder and rain had ceased and there was no wind on the face of the waters which passed in great mountains beneath the little craft. Owen, our devoted fisherman, was at the oars. Whether it took a longer or a shorter time that night to row in from the island, I do not know. But I did know then, dazed as I was, that it didn't matter—that the passing of time would never again matter to me now that there was no one to hurry to or to hurry for. We came to the place where the sea is white and you generally steer too much out of your course to avoid the shallows because of the breakers that turn to foam, and hissing and roaring roll their spray swiftly into the land.

For the first time I went close to their edge. I had no fear and I knew, dazed as I was, that never again would I be afraid, now that there was no one to shield from danger, nor in case of accident to leave behind.

As I neared the shore I saw a tall figure standing on the rocks beside our faithful chauffeur. I was not conscious of the long hours they must have been there at Magheraroarty, after motoring from the distant junction, waiting for Kingsley and me to row over from the island. I was only conscious that Fate had granted me this one boon (as if it had been in the plan) that AE of all the people left in the world was holding out his hand to help me out of the boat on to the land which in a flash had become a stretch of emptiness greater than the sea. I said, "Kingsley will not return tonight." As we drove off in the car I broke the silence again—"Kingsley will never return."

Then I told him that in the morning he had gone out ahead of me and it must have been to the cliffs above the sea and he must have drowned. And the springtide ebbing (it was the time of the summer moon) and the strong off-shore wind blowing, must have swept his body out to sea, while a storm had come up bringing thunder, lightning and rain. Although Owen, Pat and I had searched all day long and into the night we had found no trace of him.

The chauffeur's hands shook nervously as I talked. The car zig-zagged along the lonely country road that was hung high between the ocean and the Donegal mountains, now a dark irregular outline beyond the racing clouds. We had motored half of the fifteen miles that lie between Glenveagh Castle and Magheraroarty before AE turned and said in tones more tender than I have ever heard (this comes to me in the memory of sound), "Lucy, we must notify the Civic Guards. Do you know where their nearest station is?" The chauffeur did, so we turned and drove back some five miles and on down the coast, that we might tell the Guards and instruct them about continuing next morning the search for Kingsley's body. But no physical sign of him was ever again to be found. And now that the sea had become his sepulchre I was released from the dread of it which had haunted me, as it haunted the mainland women. This fear which had always hung upon me suddenly dropped and let me free.

The following afternoon (it happened to be Sunday) AE was beside me as we motored back to the coast to meet the Civic Guards at the home of Owen McGee, who was waiting for us on the road-side. His eyes were open wide like those of a frightened animal—a look men who live close to nature sometimes wear.

Kind Mrs. McGee had thrown up her arms on seeing me, ready to wail her woe. My tearless face dissuaded her. She sat down quietly on a stool beside me sobbing softly. It had not occurred to her to clean up her house for our coming. Their one-room modern shanty with a partitioned-off space was as disorderly and messy as ever. But as Kingsley had said of the McGee family, "Where there is such a spirit of love in a home why look at anything else?" Like all real people they were just themselves. Only now something new was added to their devotion—sorrow at the loss

17

of "Kingsley", as the fishermen all called him. The three
large overgrown McGee children—the oldest an epileptic—
giggling from embarrassment or curiosity, blotted out most
of the light by filling the doorway. Chickens, picking up
crumbs and from time to time making dirtier the muddy
floor, strutted about in front of the comforting ever-
burning turf fire.

As the Sergeant of the Civic Guards was away for the
week-end, his subaltern, accompanied by another young
guard, had arrived ready to fill out the questionnaire. Spelling and writing were difficult to him and nil with Owen so
it ended by AE's practically conducting this preliminary
inquest.

Once back at the castle again AE took charge of all the
details that now sprang up like rank weeds around us. I
was not surprised by the way he smoothed my spirit, but
his sure touch in matters of formality and in worldly questions was unexpected. I smile as I remember one difficulty
he had—to accustom himself to the constant cabling. "Why
waste so much money?" he would say. And when I asked
if this or that telegram made sense, not trusting myself, he
always replied, "But why say so much—why not just say
'writing'?"

He would read evenings to me from *The Avatars* as I lay
on the sofa before the turf fire. The scurrying clouds were
reflected from across the lake in the mirror above the
carved marble mantel. Sitting on the very edge of a large,
comfortable upholstered arm-chair, so that I felt he would
surely slip off, he would read until he had to stop to light

18

the lamp. Then he would continue, peering at me from time to time over the top of his spectacles, tenderly as a mother, hoping I had fallen asleep—I hoping he would think so. That book I think I shall never open again lest the star that awakened the golden-haired avatar, the little boy in the attic bedroom of the thatched cottage, should shine less bright and become more like the star-burst-ray that strikes down in such an orderly manner over the manger in the nativity paintings of the quattrocento. This was a burning, glowing star that filled the darkness above the little house. The child answering its call ran leaping joyfully over the ancient flat mountain tops that rose out of the lake just below my window, carrying his halo of light and glory into their night.

*2 Remington Lane*

*Houston, Texas*

3

12

30

*My dear Mrs. Porter.* You line has been forwarded here to me. I shall be very glad indeed to stay with you when in Boston. But I do not know what engagements have been made for me or what I have to do when I get to Boston. At present I only know the lectures I have to deliver up to 20th. Dec. I will know when I get to New York what engagements have been made for me by the committee who brought me over or by Pond who fills up the vacant dates between the economic lectures I deliver. . . . But now I know nothing so could not fix any dates. It is very kind of you to ask me to stay with you and I will be glad to see you and Mr. Kingsley Porter again. I have travelled thousands of miles since I came to U.S.A. in September, been over all the northern states in Middle West and from Seattle down to San Diego through Arizona (a marvellous country) and am here for a couple of days after which I go northwards to New York stopping here and there. It is rather tiring this perpetual travelling and speaking for one of my years. I would like to go into a hermitage for six months after my return to Ireland. I find myself thinking

20

of Donegal which is so quiet after New York, Chicago, Los Angeles, Seattle and other cities here, and pictures of the Strand at Marble Hill entice me

or pictures of the hills

Yours ever
'AE'

*17 Rathgar Avenue*

*Dublin*

$\dfrac{\begin{array}{c} 30 \\ 7 \end{array}}{31}$

*Dear Kingsley*

I gave Bregazzi the pictures to pack and send on to you.
. . . It was a great delight to be at Glenveagh. I do not
wonder at your love for the place. You are both dears and
the kindest of kind folk. I am getting rid of a mountain of
correspondence which piled up here for me. Lord what a
heap! I look at it in despair and revile the fiend who invented post offices.

Yours ever

AE.

*Dear Kingsley.* Bergin went off a week ago to the wilds of Kerry to the most remote barbaric Gaelic speaking district. I do not know where he is, but will leave the letter at his house asking it to be forwarded. If his housekeeper is on holidays in the absence of her lord and master I will try the National University. That means there will be some delay as I fancy Kerry is as slow in its posts as Glenveagh.

The delay about the pictures is due to the framing. I went round and found yesterday that they actually had put the frames together in spite of the framer's Italian tendency to dolce far niente. He promised me they would go by the end of this week. They may have gone today. At any rate I will see him tomorrow and see what swiftness winged words can impart.

It has been raining here today in a fashion Donegal could not beat. The skies wept as if their heart was broken and then they went on sniffling like a child which has cried its utmost and goes on softly weeping just for momentum's sake. I never remember weather like this before. I think I would like to commit suicide so that I might see God face to face and tell Him what I think about his slackness in running the universe He set up. I know you think grey mists and rain and mud are delicate never-sufficiently-to-be-admired harmonies; but I think you have never got over the habit of thinking all the works of the Almighty are first class. I suppose there were Greeks who admired the hexameters in which the oracles of Apollo were delivered. They were hypnotised by the name of the Deity, and I think you believe Heaven can do no wrong in Donegal.

I have started on my next book, roughly written four chapters and in a vague way see its ultimate shape and dominating mood. I will have the devil of a time making my thoughts clear to myself, and it will mean endless re-writing. But there it is. We have the passion to do a thing well and endure all kinds of discomforts for this end.

I have been reading the "Education of Henry Adams." I began it years ago but went from the house where I started it and now I find it fascinating, though I think the young Adams overdoes his own imbecility in youth which is due to the idea of being modest in writing an autobiography. He ought to have had some of Emerson's cheerful conviction that he was God himself and it would have made Adams a great man. He would never have become God quite but he would have come near the stature of an Archangel like Emerson and talked like one maybe, as Emerson sometimes did. There is no news here. All my cronies are on holidays—Yeats, Bergin, Joseph O'Neil, Con Curran, Michael O'Donovan, and I am going round to-night to see if Gogarty is left. We had a week of fine weather for the Horse Show. I hope you got some of it in Donegal. It would have served you right for your disgusting loyalties to rain, mist and general gloom in the heavens. Please give

my best wishes to Mrs. Porter. I hope the pictures will
arrive safely, as I know what the Donegal railway is I told
Bregazzi to insure them.

Yours ever

AE

*Dear Kingsley.* I am glad the pictures arrived safely. I was dubious about that Donegal railway. I remember how a parcel of mine went up and down for a week between Londonderry and Burtonport as nobody thought of dropping it out at Dunfanaghy Rd. and it was only after many wires that it came at last. I hope the pictures will not prove too tiresome possessions.

Bergin is still in the wilds of Kerry I think. . . . When he comes back I will ask him about the Keating story. Perhaps it could be solved, your problem, at the folklore institute in Christiana where they have collected I understand, all the folk lore of the planet, and have thousands of variants of folk tales in all countries. When I am next down town I will call in at the National Library and see whether Dr. Best can answer your question. It may be more in his line than Bergin's.

I have started the seventh chapter in a new book. I rough them out to get the shape of the book clear and then when I have roughed out twenty chapters I will take each sentence and agonize over it until it is clear and shapely as I can make it. If the sun would only shine a little I am sure it would have a good effect on the writing. Yet I doubt if I could stand even three months of undiluted sunshine. I vary writing which is heavy work with painting a little which is light work. You see I never know how bad my painting is as I am not learned enough and I know only too well what good writing is to find writing an easy or pleasant occupation.

Yes I expect to hear at any time that our pretty Jean has linked herself up with some fortunate young man. She ought to be multiplied and placed as ornaments about rooms and in woods. If ever in the future cycles I become a divinity a hundred million years from this and have charge of a planet I will create plenty of lovely people. It will be the aesthetic planet, and ugliness will be its crime. I must get back to my seventh chapter, and break its back before one of your countrywomen comes here from the American minister's where she is staying. A Mrs. Hart from Washington. I wish I could get the seventh chapter done. It is the very devil. Kind regards to Mrs. Kingsley.

Yours ever<br>AE.

*17 Rathgar Avenue*

*Dublin*

$$\frac{21}{8}$$
$$31$$

*Dear Kingsley.* I looked up Dr. Best at the National Library this morning and asked him about the tale you refer to in Keating. Yes there are earlier versions. Best wrote on this slip, I enclose the references. He is going on holidays and I tried to make him go with his wife to Dunfanaghy. If he goes I will let you know where he is staying. He is a charming fellow, very clever and a great authority. He is easier to talk to than Bergin whose mania for absolute accuracy makes him slow about answering questions. Best says Bergin probably knows more about Irish than anybody for the past four hundred years. And he is a great master. "To see him with a glance eating up a sentence and finding half a dozen mistakes is a lesson in itself". Bergin will not he tells me be back for three weeks from the remote district in Kerry where he buries himself every summer so that he can hear nothing spoken but Irish by native speakers. I hope the slip gives you the information you want.

Yours ever

AE.

*Dear Kingsley.* Food for soul and body! Thanks specially for the magnificent gift of the "Crosses and Culture of Ireland". I have been reading it with an interest I never imagined I would have in Irish Crosses. I started my study of Christianity in Ireland at the wrong end, that is, in my own time when it produced neither art nor literature and was so sterile that I could hardly imagine any period of fertility. What an immensity of labour and research went to the making of your book. All my documents when I write are in the library of my brain. And my lazy soul feels awe and admiring wonder at this work where you had to go all over the country indeed over Europe and ransack many, many volumes to get your materials. A lazy man I take off my hat to an industrious man. Perhaps if I had gone outside myself more the shelves inside myself would not have been so empty. In your gentle way I fancy you will give some disagreeable shocks to Irish orthodoxy which would have it that Rome and Armagh were loving twins and that Armagh the younger born never had the slightest difference of opinion or doctrine with its elder, but deferred on all fours before Rome. I wonder what Ireland would be like if Armagh had conquered? Which is it worse to be, tyrant or slave? The carving of Irish legendary tales

29

on the Crosses pleases me. You remember Francis Thompson

> *Teach how the crucifix can be*
> *Carven from the laurel tree*
> *The muses' sacred grove be wet*
> *With the red dews of Olivet*
> *And Sappho lay her burning brows*
> *On white Cecilia's lap of snows.*

Yet I feel with Usheen that "better was one day with Finn and his heroes than a thousand years of the Kingdom of Heaven" and I echo him when he says of Patrick, "Surely if the Kingdom of Heaven is made of men like you a wretched nation are the servants of the King of Grace". But probably the saints were not so bad at the start as I believed, taking my opinions from Usheen, and if the saints allowed Finn and his heroes to have their place with the saints and apostles they were not too bad. Your illustrations are very rich. I like Fig. 233. I hope the two old men pulling each other's beards are saints, or could it be Patrick and Usheen having a devil of a time of it? What a feeling for beautiful design there is in many of these Crosses and the carvings on them. You have certainly made a fine contribution to the culture of your adopted country.

I have been working away as my intelligence permits at my book about the psychology of poetry. That is what it is turning into. I have got about ten chapters written out and it will I think be unlike any book about poetry that I know, and I hardly know myself whether it is crazy or profound. However I can't really know until the critics have done their worst on it and if I am crazy, to know I am is the first step to sanity. I am sure Glenveagh must be at its best now. The autumn colour of trees and hills was marvellous, I remember once when I was in Donegal in October. My friend Frank O'Connor's book of stories, "Guests of the Nation", which I induced Macmillan to take, seems to be a great success with the reviewers. They speak of Turgeniev, Maupassant and one says Kipling is boyish in comparison so I feel happy in my friend's success. He is such a fine fellow. He is various too and I am to write a preface for a book of verse translations by him from old Irish. His version of "Old Woman of Beare" was magnificent. The talent of Ireland is now running into story telling. Besides O'Connor, Higgins and Clarke poets both, have taken to prose stories. We are rapidly filling up the gaps in our Anglo-Irish literature. Poetry we had in plenty and the best of plays, but no or few good stories. Now we are having them and all that remains now is philosophy, and Yeats and myself are trying to fill up that gap. Please remember me to Mrs. Kingsley.

Yours ever

A.E.

*My dear Mrs. Porter.* No. I had not seen the press cutting. I do not subscribe to a press agency. I think it would only increase egomania. Either praise or blame does it, so the less one hears about oneself the better. But thanks all the same for sending it. I don't remember anyone doing the sketch and it was not redrawn from any photograph I have memory of. I suppose Glenveagh is at its loveliest now as the weather here at least for the last month is cold and sunny. I was down at Coole Park with Lady Gregory and Yeats for a few days. The lake and woods there are very beautiful not so wild with mountains as Glenveagh but mysteriously lovely all the same. I may be going to London in a fortnight's time to see Gandhi. Two of his friends have written me he wants to see me as he had read books of mine when he was in prison and seems to have been impressed by them, though I fancy it is the economics in the "National Being" which interested him more than the "Candle of Vision" which he also studied in prison. I will go if my wife is well enough to leave. She is rather an invalid and now my son is gone to England there is nobody in the house except our servant (a good girl) but I don't like leaving her unless she is rather better than she has been. By the way, somebody suggested that one of the sculptured incidents of the man with a rod and figures about, might be Moses striking the rock. Tell Kingsley this. The natural tendency in this pious country is to look for scriptural rather than Pagan incidents. The belief is here that once the Irish were converted they were converted and Paganism had no further interest for them. This in spite of the famous dialogue between Oisin and St. Patrick. I am getting on with my book. Have roughed out fourteen chapters and rewritten six so that they might almost stand. I hope to have it finished by end of year or thereabouts. You see I am trying to work. All good wishes to you and the good man.

Yours ever<br>AE

*17 Rathgar Avenue*
*Dublin*

$$\frac{15}{12}$$
$$31$$

*My dear Mrs. Kingsley Porter*

The shawl came yesterday and I brought it down to the Adelaide, and my wife desires me to thank you for a present which was beautiful to her eyes. She is a trifle easier, can talk a little now and it is probable in another ten days or thereabouts she will be able to be moved home again. I see her every afternoon and stay there for a couple of hours. She cannot talk much but I think she likes me to be in her room. Yesterday she was able to read a little.

All this trouble prevents me being able to do any writing. One must be in good spirits to write, and I cannot now get into the mood so the new book must lapse for the present. I am sure Glenveagh must be marvellous at this time of the year. For inspiration and awakening of imagination I always thought wild midwinter in the West was better than summer. I am sure Kingsley enjoys it. He ought to start painting beginning with pastel drawings. I began that way and when I had messed about for a while I got to a stage where I was not afraid of colour and could work with the high confidence of absolute ignorance and that courage is

34

the first step to good work. Please give him my kindest regards and with many thanks for your kindness and sympathy.

Yours sincerely<br>AE.

*My dear Mrs. Kingsley Porter*

It was kind of you to send the cutting. I wish they had not got Lux's portrait sideways. It was a good picture and the slant destroys the drawing. My wife was let return home on Monday last week. But she has been in bed nearly ever since. And the doctors give me no hope of her recovery. Three or four months ought to see the end. You will understand that I am depressed and unable to write or think of anything. They operated to discover the cause of the trouble which was going on for many years. . . . But they are not hopeful. So you will understand how I feel with so much in my life slipping away from me.

I had finished a little book "Song and Its Fountains" which will be out this spring. I have corrected the proofs for Macmillan. It will annoy most of my critics I think. But I don't mind that. I have always written to please myself. I only wish I was more pleased with myself over it. As one gets older there is some blurring of the keen edge of one's mind. However I think it is nice writing. Was it you sent grapefruit? I got a crate from Texas without name of sender. And as I got a crate last year from McCullinan of Texas I wrote thanking him supposing it came from him as before. Anyway I thank you for the gift. My wife in hospital liked the grapefruit juice. But now it is difficult for her to take anything.

I hope you and Kingsley are both well. You should be in that divine world of Donegal, and I think it is more wildly lovely in winter than at other times. I spent a good part of a winter on the west in Mayo and Donegal once and know what it is like, how unearthly the earth is.

I did not read Wilson's book on the symbolists. Yes there was a time when Yeats called himself a symbolist and would have made me out to be one but I preferred mysticism to symbolism. I doubt that Joyce could come into that movement, or Eliot either. Villiers L'Isle-Adam, Mallarmé and Yeats yes, but I doubt Joyce and Eliot. However the meaning of words grows and all literature is symbolism in some fashion. I wish I could look at the Donegal mountains now. But I am tied here as you will understand. I suppose you go back soon to Boston. Good luck to both of you. I hope to see you when you return.

Yours ever<br>AE

*Dear Kingsley*

It was most kind of you to write to me. My wife died on the 3rd and I was spared and she was spared the pain of that longer drawn out dying which the doctors feared. They thought she might linger on for months, but she began to fail rapidly and I think with gratitude that there was but little suffering at the last. I was so heavy of heart that I went away by myself for a week to try to shake off the oppression, and returned here on Monday to get your letter. I am going to try writing again so soon as I can get back to myself. I am sending you a copy of "Song and Its Fountains" of which you read the first chapter in the Dublin Magazine. It would have been a better book only my mind was troubled while I was writing it and I could not bring a full concentration to bear on it. Anyhow it cannot be helped. There are I think interesting things in it here and there and I must only try to make the next book more complete.

I read "Axel's Castle". I think it a fine piece of literary criticism. The study of Yeats was good, and also of "Ulysses". I myself with an immense respect for Joyce's talent cannot read this book through. In the book which followed "Ulysses", of which fragments "Anna Livia Plurabelle" have been published, I think he gets away from life in the effort to get into it. That book and "The Apes of God" by Wyndham Lewis distress me for with prodigious talent there is no humanity. Well you have been gorged with Donegal scenery in all weathers and you still survive and love it and you are worthy of the place. I will try to get to that soul alluring county next summer. I sometimes think I will never get back to writing until I do. There is something in the air or stones or earth which kindles the imagination.

I hope things will clear up in U.S.A. The papers speak of more flutters in the stock exchange in New York, or is it Wall St., and people are buying stocks and shares with some of the old optimism. I think the disease runs deeper than Wall Street remedies. But a reaction is due from whatever cause and if U.S.A. begins to expand Europe will in a reflected glow. Please give my kindest regards to Mrs. Porter. I am writing hastily. I found on my return all the letters one receives from friends and I must answer some of them.        Yours ever

AE

*Dear Kingsley.* I got your kind letter a few days ago. I have settled down to write at my "Avatars" in a determined desultory kind of way. That is I always try to write. But as the writing depends on intuition and imagination more than industry the industrious writer has to wait while the idle psyche, or a psyche otherwise engaged, thinks fit to do its part in the work. But I guess the work will go slowly until I can once more breathe the Donegal air. Then I feel reinvigorated and after I come back the sentences run away before the industrious part of me can keep pace. I am glad you found the little book "Song and Its Fountains" of some interest. I find my reviewers pleased with it. The Observer made it the Book of the Week and Humbert Wolfe gave two columns to it. Miss Edith Sitwell called it a mysteriously beautiful book and lavished poetry on it. The Times was friendly and intelligent. The Irish papers amuse me warning their readers against my heretical and pagan mind. But I think the reviewers read it fascinated a little in spite of the strict orthodoxy which they uphold, and which I suspect is a very weak staff to lean on when they venture a little out of the ordinary thinking.

Yes I shall be glad if I am alive to go to Glenveagh when you come back to Ireland. I hope we shall not be at war with England or a blockaded country or something like that. De Valera's policy terrifies me and I confess I do not like his party or its ideals. They have not a poet among them nor do they inspire poetry, and a cause that has no poets is doomed to perish. I may be mistaken, or I may simply be getting old and stupid. I hope it is the latter for I would rather think I was getting old and stupid than that all my fellow countrymen were unintelligent.

I guess the economic advisers of almost all governments are rather quacks. Remember the hordes of eminent economists who came to the peace conference to advise statesmen how much they could extract from Germany and only one, Keynes, who resigned, was not proved a fool. I have no doubt they all went home with increased prestige and are now advising the Hoovers and MacDonalds and the French and Italian governments and the patients are dying of starvation, i.e. unemployment. I would like to think Russia was going to raise the standard of living and employ all her people, and if she did so then my temporary remedy which is to have a benevolent dictatorship on capitalist-socialist lines may be tried in despair. Of course all systems are good only for a generation. As the soul changes so must the social order. Whenever we get human kindness we will get back to the Golden Age when as the Purana says, "The minds of men shall become clear as crystal." They place the date of the return of the Golden Age about 430,000 years from this, and I think this reasonable and it inclines me to believe the old Indian as a true seer into futurity. It has been dry and frosty here for over a month and people are afraid of a drought! In Ireland! But the pent up flood will I hope come at the time of the Eucharistic Congress when as the country will be dripping with piety within it would only be congruous to have it dripping without. I do wish Providence would manifest its disapproval of such exhibitions by drowning them. When I think of all the harm that old clergyman Patrick did by his blundering zeal I can never forgive him. He and his tribe have made mush of the wits of our people. It is the Black Art. You don't believe in the Black Art. But watch the way the Church takes the young and hypnotises by suggestion until the psyche is bound stiff by terrors.

What degree are they giving you at Williams? Are you a D.C.L. or an LL.D. or a D. Litt? I am something of the kind myself and can tell you that your character will remain unaltered. If naming us things could lift us up to heaven we would all be there long ago. But I am glad they are decorating you, for it means that some people have grown to like you as you deserve to be liked.

I was in London for a few days and saw the French exhibition. There was a Courbet there of deer in a wood and an Enchanted Castle by Claude and I was filled with an infinite spirit of greed and would if I was a military dictator have seized them and also "A Jewish Merchant" by Rembrandt in the National Gallery, and with a Chinese Landscape in Washington I would have had my ideal collection, not large, I am not greedy, but choice. I dare say you will hear things about Ireland in the papers fairly soon. The British lion is slowly showing a tooth and twitching his tail. But nothing may happen. And when nothing happens that is best of all in a country. For it is in silence thought begins. All spectacular events stop thinking. The lust of the eye and the pride of life are too quickened and they obscure everything else. Please remember me to Mrs. Porter. I must close this as I have to write a preface to a life of Roger Casement and I promised it at once.

Yours ever

A.E

*17 Rathgar Avenue*

*Dublin*

30

4

*32*

*Dear Kingsley*

The paper on the "Relief of Labhraidh Loingseach"
was very interesting. As you say it tends to support
your thesis that pagan subjects were often carved on
the Irish Crosses. I think you are right in dismissing
Caibre Cat Head, who was the ancient counterpart of
the modern Bolshevist, and such folk have always been
anathema to the clerical imagination. The only thing I
quarrel with is your assumption that Ovid's poetry was dear
to school boys, unless indeed Latin verse was inculcated in
America by gentler methods than it was when I was a boy
at school and Latin poetry was an abomination to me. Even
now I dislike the Romans because their literature was im-
parted to me in such painful ways. It was only a year ago
that I found myself really enthusiastic about the Pollio (I
think it is called) of Virgil, the prophecy of the return of
the Golden Age. I was pleased to see a very good review
of "Song and Its Fountains" in the New York Times Book
Review Apl 17 which somebody sent me. It has been very
well reviewed in England by Yeats, Humbert Wolfe, and
Edith Sitwell, fellows in the craft. It seems to have revived
the ancient doctrine of poetic inspiration as something to
be gone into again.

44

I have not been getting on with my new book during the last weeks so took up painting again until the current flows once more.

We are all wondering to what catastrophe De Valera may lead us. Some folk think nothing will happen and I murmur to myself "Alas regardless of their doom the little victims play". In June we have a Eucharistic Congress and the nation will drip with piety and I will be very Rabelaisian in soul by way of contrast. But I daresay even scraps of Irish politics get across the Atlantic and you know what the New Government is up to.

You have your own troubles and from cabled news unemployment seems no less in U.S.A. I could almost imagine eternal justice had decreed that the civilians of the countries in the Great War who approved of it were to be visited with suffering equal to that endured by the men in the armies. I notice Mexico has no unemployment. It was not in the war, while Spain which kept out of the war has been blessed by a revolution which enabled it to get rid of King and Church. But I won't pursue these obscure speculations further. I only wanted to thank you for the paper and to say How d'ye do to you and Mrs. Porter.

Yours ever<br>AE.

*Dear Kingsley.* Don't talk with such an air of pride of the muddle of politics and economics in your country. We can match anything you have to show. Our new government has outraged British feeling so that our markets there are closing against us. They have piled on tariffs on everything they can think of even on books which now bring a ten percent tariff, fifteen on French, German and American books, so I warn you. The only consolation is that farmers are already beginning to curse De Valera who is ruining their market in England and at the same time he insists that they shall pay him the annuities he withholds from England. Lord what a mess! If the British have not invaded Ireland to regain the lost jewel of their empire I will go to Glenveagh on the middle of July as Mrs. Kingsley suggested. I don't expect they will invade us for I fancy after some months of independence the vast majority will want to be back in the British Commonwealth and I am not sure the Briton will want us back. If we are outside he can oppress us legally and rightfully by tariffs and get a revenue by taxing cattle, bacon, butter, a revenue which he could not get otherwise. These wild observations I make because I have met a tribe of outraged Irish who were followers of De Valera and now don't know what they are, only they

46

are sure they are not devotees of his any longer. Don't send me any books from U. S. A., not even any masterpieces of literature as I shall have to pay fifteen per cent as well as 2/6 package tax, at least so the Revenue Commissioners declare. I will take all foreign masterpieces for granted and brood over the books I am fortunate enough to possess. The Eucharistic Congress takes place in June and I want to get out of the city and its half million of imported pious folk and its ugly decorations. Was there not a pleasant little hotel at Gartan near the lake? Do you remember its correct name and address? I might run up there and paint the lake and woods while the pious are on their knees in Phoenix Park.

Lady Gregory died at midnight on Sunday night. All my generation are dropping out rapidly. There was O'Grady, Synge, Mrs. Green, Lady Gregory, Louis Claude Purser, Sir Horace Plunkett, Griffith, Susan Mitchell, and George Moore is tottering. Of my boyhood friends Yeats only is left. I contemplate with a peace I had never imagined that my turn will come fairly soon in the law of averages. But I would like to think

> *"Some work of noble note may yet be done*
> *Not unbecoming men who strive with gods."*

I look to Donegal to give me a new drink from the earth fountain of life, and I will then be able to get on with my "Avatars" which hangs at present. I am trying to paint to amuse myself and get my hand in and I even feel dim stir-

47

rings of poetry which is absurd after naming my last book of verse "Vale".

I gather things are getting worse in the States as they are I believe in England, France and Germany. My reading is that the industrial system and the agricultural system as they perfect themselves enable fewer and fewer people to produce the goods and food required. Production is perfect. Distribution is impossible in any fullness because the economic system does not enable those who profit by way of wages, salaries and dividends to buy back all that is produced. There is always an increasing surplus which must be exported. But as all countries are adopting the same system and closing their ports against imported goods this makes the unemployment worse. It is inevitable any way and must grow worse so long as people only think of perfecting production and don't try to solve the problem of consumption which can only be done by distributing somehow the means to buy back the goods produced. I fancy if capital was organised completely it could, eliminating internal competition, give the workers the benefit of shorter hours and employ the unemployed. Alternatively, but improbably, the problem could be solved by scrapping machinery as in Butler's "Erewhon" and living simply like Mexicans who have no unemployment because they have no mass production. The third alternative is Communism. Please Heaven none of these solutions will come in my time, as I hope the system will last out my life. I grew up under it and am accustomed to it. And I could not stand the highly organized machine state whether capitalist or

Communist, and I would feel horribly uncomfortable in a Mexican world of primitive cobblers and weavers. I suppose every soul fits the social order it is fitted for. I can't imagine any country or place quite so fitted for my failings as my own country and my own location. I don't think I would have liked the sanitary arrangements in ancient Athens though I would have delighted in the society of Plato and Aristophanes and Socrates. I believe the smells in Chinese cities are worse and that disposes of a yearning to have lived close to Laotze. I have read accounts of Hindu yogis and I cannot with my temperament see myself with a beggar's bowl following after Buddha. I love his wisdom but not his manner of living. Yes, I am where I ought to be, the imperfect peg in the imperfect hole which it fits perfectly. The Lord has provided for my frailties by his choice of time and place and intellectual environment. He has even provided a Kingsley Porter to make me aware of a lovely lake, unknown hitherto to my life and I am a connoisseur in lakes. When I think over my life I do not fear facing God. I murmur to myself the wisdom of Omar Khayyam

*"Pish!*
*He's a good fellow and 'twill all be well."*

I ramble on like this in sheer desperation because I dare not think too intently on my country as I know I would get miserable, so I whistle to keep up courage and turn my eyes away. I am not really melancholy. I find myself in deep

49

peace inside only outwardly I rage and gesticulate and curse the fools who run my country. I gather from your letter that you are cursing the fools who run yours. So when we meet we shall make a pessimistic duet and get quite cheerful over the art we show in sadness. Please give my kind regards to Mrs. Porter and thank her for her note.

Yours ever<br>AE.

*17 Rathgar Avenue* ·
*Dublin*                      *Friday [July 8, '32]*


*My dear Mrs. Porter*
  So you have managed to get back to Ireland and broke through our customs barriers. I thought our New Government had tariffs prohibitive of everything. Perhaps they forgot Americans. They have forgotten nothing else. I will on my part essay to break through the barriers set up by the Northern Government on Friday next the 15th and come to you on that date. At the moment I am trying to get some canvases and stretchers through our unspeakable customs but do not think that they will not get through or delay me. I will write again next week saying precisely what time my train gets to Letterkenny. I have not at the moment a railway guide by me. It will be a great pleasure to see you and Kingsley again. I suppose he is looking out hopefully for a rainy and misty day, esoteric luxuries for the senses which he cannot get in Boston. I will defer discussing anything until I come.

                    Yours ever
                      AE.

*17 Rathgar Avenue*
*Dublin*

$$\frac{8}{7}$$
*32*

*Dear Mrs. Porter.* I have succeeded in getting some canvas, paints and stretchers and can now say definitely I will leave Dublin for your part of the country on Friday next the 15th. I have also got a railway guide and it tells me that I can get to Letterkenny at 5.35 in the afternoon. I trust the railway guide. I hope my trust is well founded, for I am going to start that day and trust myself to trains which I hope will run to schedule. I once wired to a hotel in Dungloe to get a car to meet me at Burtonport at 9.30, my train got in at a quarter past 12 that night and my car had gone believing that no train was coming. This was mid-winter and the snow on the ground. However I saw a car outside the station and jumped in it telling the man to drive like blazes. It was only when I got to Dungloe that I found I had taken somebody else's car and I sent him back to take up that unfortunate man from the icy cold station. You see I start with hope chastened by experience. But I daresay it will be all right. Mostly it is all right. I am happy at the thought of seeing you all again.

Yours ever

AE.

*17 Rathgar Avenue*

*Dublin*                    *Tuesday [August 23, '32]*

*Dear Kingsley.* . . . Since I came back I found it very difficult to settle down to write and only last evening I took up the MSS. of my "Avatars" and wrote a little. I will try now to stick to it and I only hope the subject will stick to me, i.e. that the tide of ideas which flowed so easily when I began will continue to flow and not sink into the subconscious the way Lady Gregory's lake at Coole had a habit of sinking into the hole at the end of the lake. We got the tail end of your Ulster thunderstorm, a good deal of rumbling and a few flashes but nothing like what was reported in the papers about Donegal and other Ulster Counties where whole villages sat up all night saying their prayers, telling their beads and other magical practises to control the elements. I would like to teach them the real philosophy of magic. But if I went to any pious Catholic village and said, "You folks, I hear you believe in magic, you have been practising incantations against thunder and lightning. Now the real way to work the thing is this". I would be stoned as a pagan, for the poor dears do not know they were trying to practise magic—and that a thousand years from this when Catholicism is only an historical legend, learned scholars at Harvard and elsewhere will be publishing the prayers as ancient magic formulae and runes

53

and incantations. . . . I remember once quarreling with Yeats who was walking around the room with a sword in one hand muttering spells to ward off evil spirits and I noticed that every time he passed a plate of plums he put down his unoccupied hand and took a plum and I said, "Yeats you cannot evoke great spirits and eat plums at the same time", and he insisted he could. . . . Yeats was in his youth when he ate the plums and has learned more about the fitness of things. . . . There is no other news to tell. I believe the only news of any interest does not come from the great cities or from the councils of state, but from some lonely watcher on the hills who has a momentary glimpse of infinitude and feels the universe rushing at him. I got from U.S.A. a life of Emerson by Van Wyck Brooks who sent it to me. It is written with reverence. But Emerson is not merciful to his biographers as Byron, Shelley, Oscar Wilde and others were. There is no incest to chronicle, no sodomy, no running away with girls, no prisons. All his adventures were in his soul, and one might deduce them if one was as great as Emerson and if they could be told they would be far more exciting than Byron's affair with his half sister or Shelley's troubles with girls. But I must not weary you with my bad handwriting. Please give my kind regards to my ever kind hostess at Glenveagh and also to your two guests from Spain if they are still with you.

Yours ever

AE

P.S. I discovered after writing, I was out of ordinary envelopes and had to use this which will make you think you are receiving a summons to attend a jury or notice of a libel action or some affair of the world like that.

*Dear Kingsley*

I think with envy of you in your Donegal seclusion. Here I am immersed in the honorary secretaryship of the new Irish Academy of Letters. I drew up the rules and got them registered for Yeats who immediately made a speech which has caused the usual commotion. The Irish Press had an angry leader about the Academy. It is not the right kind of Academy. Its membership is alien to true Irish ideals, and it suggests somehow another Academy could be formed of the right kind of men of genius which would be in accord with true Irish nationality. Only they don't give a single name and indeed it would be hard to find them when the invitations to membership include Shaw, Yeats, George Moore, James Joyce, James Stephens, Stephen MacKenna, Dunsany, Lennox Robinson, Sean O'Casey, Seamus O'Sullivan, Austin Clarke, F. R. Higgins, Liam O'Flaherty, Lawrence (of Arabia), Helen Waddell, Miss Summerville, Peader O'Donnell, Francis Stuart, St. J. Ervine, T. G. Murray, Padraic Colum, Sean O'Faolain, Oliver Gogarty, Douglas Hyde, Stephen Gwynn, L. A. G. Strong, AE, and I think a couple of others whose names I can't remember at the moment. We will probably be severe critics of the censorship. The last book condemned is Austin Clarke's

"Bright Temptation" which I suggested you should read. If you have not, it is late now for Ireland. But it will probably do this beautiful book good elsewhere. As for politics we exist in a kind of trance unable to move or do anything. I guess there will be a general crumbling everywhere. I see things are going no better in your country and some prophesy nearly twenty million unemployed in two years' time. But I imagine if it gets that far the twenty million will be employed in revolution. I don't write this to make you gloomy. But I remember your liking for artistically complete pictures of decay. I try to keep cheerful by writing poetry. I find to my astonishment that lyrics come every now and then with the old ease. I scribble one on the back page which pleased me for a kind of wandering rhythm. If your friend Sachs notifies me he is in Dublin I will be glad to see him. Isn't it wonderful Gandhi threatening to starve himself to death if the untouchables do not have something done for them by the Hindus? And they in a flurry lest his death be on their shoulders summoning meetings! Could any European or American starve himself and affect public policy? He would be put in an asylum. There must be great national gentleness in India. With kind regards to both of you.

Yours ever<br>AE

## Magic

*O dark holy magic,*
*To steal out at dawn,*
*To dip face and feet in grasses*
*The dew trembles on*
*Ere its might of spirit healing*
*Be broken by the dawn.*

*O to reel drunken*
*With the heady dew,*
*To know again the virgin wonder*
*That boyhood knew,*
*While words run to music, giving voices*
*To the voiceless dew.*

*They will make, those dawn-wandering*
*Lights and airs,*
*The bowed worshipping spirit*
*To shine like theirs,*
*They will give thy lips an aeolian*
*Music like theirs.*

A.E.

*Dear Kingsley.* Why moan over the crossing of the Channel and the inconveniences of travel when the air line will take you from London to Paris in 4 hours and the customs examination is light. I suppose that would be an adhesion to the mechanical age which would seem to you almost as bad as Bolshevism. I fancy you sigh for travels with a donkey like Stevenson's. I knew two Americans who travelled round Ireland with a donkey carrying their packs. They were both artists. They seemed to enjoy it. Of course crossing the Channel you would have to get the steamer. But think of the delight of strapping your pack on your donkey's back and striding along to your churches and tombs. What a nice book you could write "Adventures of an Archaeologist with a Donkey". Perhaps as your relics grew in number you would have to increase the number of donkeys from one to a caravan. I like suggesting such things to my friends, my impish nature impels me to bring them up against themselves. I am sure with all your yearning for a simpler age without mechanics you could not endure it. You really ought to thank Heaven that you being born in a comfortable age can investigate uncomfortable ages without their dirt, smells, bad cooking, lack of sanitation etc. I wonder would you in the world of Abelard or

Columcille have felt much different from Mark Twain's Yankee at the Court of King Arthur. The age we are born in fits us really like a glove. There is no news here except that our politicians grow more insane in their economics. At present they are taxing us to give bounties on exports to England. We live badly to enable our eternal enemies to live cheaply and get our bacon, eggs, butter, meat, etc. cheaper than we can get them ourselves. And while we heap these benefits on them we cry out against them, and then tax imports from England so that everything here may be dearer and we may come more quickly to wear the hair-shirt of the self torturing ascetics. The "Avatars" drags its slow body along. I write it more slowly than any other book because I grow doubtful about myself. This may be age partly and partly wisdom. Odd verses come up, a little painting and that's all. Getting old is a sleepy and not un-comfortable business. Yeats is in U.S.A. James Stephens returns from your land, but, alas, not to Ireland. Frank O'Connor is my consolation for other departed friends. I hope to carry him along with me to Dunfanaghy next year if the country is not by that time in chaos. My dog, my cat, my maid and myself are well. All sleepy except my maid who has to keep wide awake to look after the rest of us. In rare moments of spirit-waking I write a sentence or a verse. This which I call a mountain tarn was begun at Glenveagh, the first verse, the rest I finished here.

*The pool glowed to a magic cauldron*
*O'er which I bent alone.*
*The sun burned fiercely on the waters,*
*The setting sun,*
*A madness of fire: around it*
*A dark glory of stone.*

*O mystic fire!*
*Stillness of earth and air!*
*That burning silence I*
*For an instant share.*
*In the crystal of quiet I gaze*
*And the God is there.*

*Within that loneliness*
*What multitude!*
*In the silence what ancient promise*
*Again renewed!*
*Then the wonder goes from the stones*
*The lake and the shadowy woods.*
                              AE.

Kind regards to Mrs. Porter. How would she like travelling
with a donkey?

*Dear Kingsley.* I went round last evening to Frank O'Connor. He will gladly come if he can get away. But is not certain that he can. You see he has charge of the Pembroke Library and he got three months leave in the summer on a doctor's recommendation as he had some stomach trouble and he is doubtful about trying to get a week even. However he will do his best. You would like him. He is the most natural charming fanciful young man of genius I know and his book on the Gaelic culture will I think be delightful reading. He is working hard at it.

I am glad you liked the poem. It is difficult to get into words a mood that inhabits you for a moment so that you seem to have gone into eternity and come out in a second of time.

Yes I can imagine how beautiful the lake is in winter. I once spent a whole winter in the west of Mayo, Galway, Donegal and Kerry from October to March and the wild skies seemed every moment to be opening doors into eternal being. I don't think Roosevelt will make any difference. I doubt if the victory of Hoover would have made any difference. I have long got past the idea that the heads of states except once in a thousand years are really the shepherds of millions. They are swept along by the rest. That they seem to march in the first rank is nothing. They have to go on or they would be crushed so they keep in step. Russia will be all right in twenty-five years when the younger generation of Communists begins to fill up the spiritual vacancy that nature abhors. They will do it little dream by dream until suddenly they will have discovered the spiritual counterpart to Communism. The poor English are going to have a bad time of it. They have not imagination enough to find a way out and they are too decent for bloodshed, the crude revolutionary way, or I imagine they are so. But are you not a little unjust in attributing to them the origin of prohibition? O dear man, all they did was to water their beer in the war. But you in America! How can you? Woman suffrage yes, employers' liability yes. But prohibition and high wages no. These are in your account whether they be bad or good things. Our Academy has been perfectly constructed to be unacademic. It contains all the wild young men of talent, and there is a special rule suggested by G.B.S. that nobody can in future be elected if by his election it would raise the average age of academicians beyond sixty. I would have put the average at fifty myself, then all the old men like Yeats, Shaw, myself would be forced to look for the young. I would have written a better reply to Father Gannon only I was stuffed up with a bad cold while I was writing it. If I had been clear in my head I would have played with him beautifully I think. But there it is the product of a bad cold in head and chest. That's almost gone now and I am beginning to feel a resurrection of my wits. I don't know what's going to happen in Ireland. All at sea about it. But it won't be placidly dull anyhow though it may be stupidly exciting. Kind regards to Mrs. Porter.

Yours ever

AE

*Dear Kingsley*. The repetition of rhyme was done deliber-
ately. I get tired sometimes of the rhyme and prefer the
surprise of repetition which of course is not a new thing
in poetry. "He lay down like a lion, like a young lion", or
Poe,

> *"And now while so quietly*
> *Lying, it fancies*
> *A holier odour about it of pansies*
> *Of rue and the beautiful*
> *Puritan pansies."*

There were a great many word rhymes to maintain a unity
of sound, "magic" and "grasses" are in assonance in the
Gaelic fashion and are so used instead of rhymes.
"Drunken" and "wonder" are related in the same way. It
was technically an experiment in new rhythms. Spiritually
it could be understood by those who remember what
Krishna says in the Bhagavad-Gita, "I am the sweet smell in
the earth, the brightness in the fire". That is that nothing
exists without that element of divinity in it somewhere, so
that dawn, winds, dew, earth, grasses to the spiritual mind
reveal their own participation in that spirit.

I was reading T. S. Eliot's just published collection of essays on criticism, very sound, a little arid and dry. The best thing in it the study of Dante which is the best thing I have read in English on that poet.

I wonder why your American friends are optimistic about its economics. I cannot see at present any reason why things should get better there than why they should get better in England. In no country do the producers distribute enough in wages, salaries and profits to enable those who get them to buy back what is produced and in every country the mechanization of industry enables fewer people to produce the goods and food required by the rest, so that unemployment becomes inevitable under our present economic system. Of course if prohibition is removed it will add to the revenue of the states, as I assume they will tax alcohol virtuously, to show that it is still regarded as an evil luxury. But brewers and distillers employ in proportion to the money spent in them fewer people than almost any other kind of industry. The articles, whiskey and the like, are made so expensive by heavy duties excise that people in buying these support fewer workers than they do when buying boots, clothes or other untaxed commodities. It is quite possible that more people are employed at present in bootlegging, a difficult thing under peril of legal interference, than might be employed if the industry could be legally carried on in breweries and distilleries. I do not press this doubt. But certainly people now engaged in carrying on a vast subterranean industry will be out of a job when Prohibition is removed and I doubt whether the spirit of adventure in bootlegging will qualify these engaged in it to become manufacturers later on. However this may be my pessimistic spirit. I liked your hearty hatred of the Democrats, and I think it must be that you are one of those born Republicans. You remember Thackeray's [*sic*] lines?

> *"Every child that is born alive*
> *Is either a little Liberal*
> *Or else a little Conservative."*

Your faith in your party has survived the economic debacle and it is therefore the very grain of your being. I think I have got rid of the pain of opposites in myself and look philosophically on the two parties in Ireland without affection for either. It is a great comfort having nothing to attack or defend. I have just read a quite good book "Sketches in Criticism" by Van Wyck Brooks one of the best American critics. I think I will suggest to him to form an American Academy of Letters to fix high standards. But I hesitate wondering where he would get his first "Forty Immortals", twenty would be enough for a beginning and even they would be hard to get. The trouble about literary movements in any country is this that there are only two or three writers of genius and they generally hate each other because they see different eternities. Kind regards to Mrs. Porter.

Yours ever

AE.

*Dear Mrs. Porter*

I have a rather ancient railway guide and it tells me that I can get to Letterkenny at 5.35 P.M. I imagine it is correct for I have been getting there at that time for years past. But tomorrow I will enquire at Cooks and assure myself that I am right. If I am wrong I will write again. On Monday next since you are so kind I will go to Letterkenny. I am sorry Frank O'Connor cannot come. He cannot get away from his library. He had hoped to be able as he had applied for the post of librarian in Cork and he thought it would be decided in the middle of December and he would be free to leave Pembroke and come with me. But the inevitable delays which attend all democratic decisions have brought it about that the librarian for Cork will be appointed in the new year. I am hoping Frank does not get it as he is one of my most attractive friends, and I don't think he cares very much. Cork supplies the raw material of characters for histories. Dublin supplies an intelligent society in which I am afraid from all accounts Cork is sadly deficient. I am sorry he is not coming as you would have liked him greatly and Kingsley would have been delighted I think with his ideas for the book on Irish culture which Frank is writing. Any how Frank promised me he would try to

68

get to Donegal next summer. I have told him that Cork and Kerry are obvious in comparison, whatever merits they may have in supplying disreputable characters for a story teller. It is thirty years since I saw Donegal in the winter and I am longing to see it again, and also to see and talk with two kind friends at Glenveagh, and I have also the hope that the earth may whisper to me some more lyrics. I am sure Kingsley has a masterpiece of pessimism completed over Franklin Roosevelt's lordship of the States. I have not been lonely enough to put up the structure of a rival masterpiece about Ireland. There are too many pros and cons about me to permit of a confident structure. But if Kingsley can only be cheered by an artistic pessimism I have some sketchy ideas with merit from that point of view. I have always been in hot water and a letter I wrote in the Irish Times, December 13, has made much blood boil. I was even called the Irish Mephistopheles by a young Republican who a week afterwards heroically withdrew the title and said what made him so angry was that nature had intended me to be the Irish Claudel and I had eluded my destiny. I had to rush into this controversy as Yeats is in U.S.A. When he returns he will supply all the noble indignation required for the defence of the Irish Academy of Letters. Kingsley does not like academies I fear and he will sympathize rather with the enemy. But I wrote to an American literary friend who was lamenting about the state of American criticism and I suggested he should start an American Academy of Letters and if he takes my advice Kingsley can fight happily against such a monster in his own country. I don't think I have anything more to say except that the efficiency of American fountain pens is greatly overrated. The one with which I am writing doles out the ink like a miser and yet I have had it for five or six years and have treated it like a gentleman and written quite good poems with its reluctant aid. So good-by until Monday next.

Yours ever

AE.

P.S. I found it was unjust to the pen, I forgot to unscrew it a little to let the ink flow. It is a first class pen of excellent American efficiency.

19
—
33

17 Rathgar Av
Dublin..

Dear Kingsley, This sketch is not 17
Rathgar avenue where my body is at
present, but a memory of Glenveagh
where I went in my mind when
I thought of writing. You & Lucy
were most delightful & friendly of
hosts. You have come back to
see the birth of "Technocracy" in your
country, a terrible name, the
camouflage of science which is to
be the new religion of the world
with the engineers as its outposts
and advance troops. I hear that
they offer to every American family

I would like to know, if the rumour of Technocracy has been ever ... in ... in U.S.A. about ... about ... You ... will mean that the Technocrats have you not ... . If ... it's ... you have never heard of them, ... you know? I ... will not be a market-... to say ... ? a ... . But ... not ... you many how? ... explain how a ... in the Technocrats state I ... not except. But ... was in ... know what will in the ... . I ... about will hardly as in Heric from the ...

the equivalent of twenty thousand dollars a year of the families will bow down & worship them. The echoes of the Technocrats ideas have been heard on this side, the papers who went & the public even lifting their heads out of the despondency as the burglar Ronny wobbling endless beer bottles in Dunsanys stealing gates lifts his head for a moment as the other burglar tries to open the gates of heaven with "old nut cracker". It's difficult here to know just how seriously the American public take the ideas of the Technocrats. Is it the interest of cinema goers in a new sensation, or has the idea really found supporters among the wise & well informed. If you ever have time to drop a line

Spanish queen her called the two theologians who wrangled & squabbled for days in the court and who replied to the King who asked her what she thought "They are both in rotten bad condition". I am working again at the Avatars. with a mild enthusiasm. feeling that there are too many books in the world, and the only use of mine is to keep my own mind alive. Are you not already skating on the lake and your afternoon walk through mud & storm. Kind regards to both from him

AE

*17 Rathgar Avenue*
*Dublin.*

$$\frac{4}{2}$$
$$33$$

*Dear Lucy*

It was nice to hear from you. I do not imagine a stormy Atlantic crossing is the best time to study "The Dream of Ravan". But I am glad you have got it. It is really a very profound book under all its fantasy and Indian scholars have told me that it penetrates deeper into an understanding of Indian mysticism than the work of any other European interpreter. I owe a great deal to it. Probably after Whitman you will not find Carpenter very exciting though there are fine symbolic poems in "Towards Democracy" like the "Secret of Time and Satan."

Our election is over and nobody knows what use De Valera is going to make of his majority. If he bribes labour enough he can keep in for a long time. The question is whether he can find funds for the unsatiable Labour Party without losing other support just as necessary. Labour seems to believe that there is an inexhaustible fund to draw upon. But you can't take more out of a hat than you put into it. And I doubt if the annual wealth created in Ireland was shared out evenly between all individuals that it would give one pound a week to everybody. But what reason is there to meditate on the state of Ireland when you have America in as bad a way on a more gigantic scale. You have two countries in a bad way tied round your neck! Whereas I have only one. I won't write about Ireland more or depress Kingsley who staggers gloomily under the weight of U.S.A. and Cole's Guide, which is I think a very good guide to economic reality. I myself think economics, politics, and all the externalities depend on the spiritual state of humanity. The universe is moved from within just as we are ourselves. And it is the sum total of our being its balance between light and darkness which begets our varying fortunes on the outside. Any system would be endurable if there is good will. An autocracy could be endured if the Despotism was truly benevolent. An aristocracy so long as the principle of noblesse oblige is living can be endured. Even an oligarchy if there is the spirit of human kindness in it will be acceptable. Kindness is the power which unites things otherwise incompatible. It is our hatreds, national and personal, engendered in the deeps of our being that ooze outward and make wars and dislocations in society. I am sure if one had omniscience to see into all human affairs it would be found that the final

76

cause of this or that disorder was somebody with a bad heart and a bad temper, and Emerson's idea of a moral cause for all troubles and ailments would be found to be true. Oliver Gogarty is in your country at present. I wonder will he come to Boston. Yeats has just returned with promises of money for his Academy of Letters and an increased power of irritating his Catholic countrymen here. In fact I imagine his power in this respect begins to rival my own. I am tugging away at the "Avatars". I have three more chapters to block out and then I must rewrite it all carefully. Sometimes I think it might be good and at other times I think it dreadful. But it is the only way of keeping one's soul alive to be doing something which requires one to use intuition and imagination. When we create, says Simon Magus, we are closest to the high gods whose attribute is to create. Simon says we have all the powers of the high gods in latency and by creating we grow like them and into their being. I am experimenting in his philosophy. A little too late in life perhaps. But better luck next life! Kind regards to Kingsley.

Yours ever

AE.

*Dear Kingsley*

I look across the Atlantic feeling that Hollywood dominates your country. It could only be in the cinema that those swift dramatic changes in politics had their inspiration. In a week no banks open their doors. Multimillionaires cannot cash a cheque. In another week prohibition is dead. Beer appears on every table. What was criminal is now virtuous. What next? If thirteen million unemployed suddenly found jobs it would not be incredible. But I am afraid it is impossible. Did President Roosevelt go to the cinema every night? Was it there he found the swift, the cinema-way to the American heart? He is the Douglas Fairbanks of politics, the swift athlete. Can he keep it up? Even Hitler has nothing on him. Ireland appears the silent screen in comparison. Will De Valera take a hint? I hope not. I write now with wonder to you. But by the time you get this your astonishing President may have brought off half a dozen fresh exploits and the closed banks, the frothing beer may appear as remote history. I thought of possible exploits, a war with Japan to get the unemployed out of the country and get them killed off in Manchuria, a law insisting that every American citizen drinks a gallon of Whiskey every month, duty-paying whiskey so that the revenue may expand with pleasure alike to the taxpayer and the tax-receiver. These extravagant adventures loom up before my mind as possibly taking place and I feel very aged and quiet and belonging to a very old world. A survivor of the Golden Age.

But there, I won't annoy you any more anticipating Roosevelt's future policies. I am really in high spirits because I finished writing "Avatars" and sent the MSS. to the typists. When I get it back I may have to rewrite it all over or tear it up in a rage. But at least I completed it in a fashion and if it does not read too bad when I get it back I will try to make the writing as good as I can. I am since last evening when I finished the MSS. trying to imagine myself writing another book. But I'll let ideas germinate in my mind for a little before I think of anything else. I don't suppose there is much more in me. Yeats and I confessed to each other that we had done our work and anything else we might do would be merely multiplying shadows of ourselves. Still I have a queer adventure in post mortem psychology in my mind which might be made terrible and beautiful if I could conjure up enough energy in my soul to write it. But I won't start hastily on anything. At present I am feeling an interest in the future of the planet and its children. And I have two friends who are astrologers and who tell me what is going to happen next year in Ireland, in Europe, in the world, and I steer my way by believing the exact opposite of what they tell me. This you may say shows a credulity about astrology which is inexcusable in a man of intelligence, to assume that the opposite is always

79

true is to believe in a negative science of the stars. But if you knew my two friends and had listened for years to their astrological predictions you would like myself come to believe that the exact opposite would always happen. Do you yourself whenever a politician, or financial expert or banker in your country makes a prophecy believe anything he says will happen? No, from past experience of optimistic prophesyings from such experts, whenever they say prosperity is round the corner you shudder and tighten your belt and tell Lucy to lay up a stock of tinned foods to prepare for the worst. Or if you don't you prove yourself incapable of learning from experience. Why even a Wall St. friend of mine knows enough to guide himself by believing the opposite of all the experts tell him. This as you see is not a serious letter. It is only to let you know I am alive and a little hilarious having finished the MSS. Give my best good wishes to Lucy.

Yours ever

AE.

17 Rathgar Avenue

Dublin

18
5
33

Dear Kingsley

Here you are blaming England for all your woes when the English are just poor muddled people like all the other people governing the planet. Do you really think Ramsay MacDonald or Baldwin or Simon or Chamberlain have more brains than Roosevelt or Hoover? They are all really forceful mediocrities put in power or place because the nations demand mediocrities, i.e. people who are intelligible and who don't say things the people can't understand. The English never trusted Disraeli because he had a touch of genius and when Arthur Balfour injudiciously showed he had a subtle brain the word went round "B.M.G.", which being interpreted meant "Balfour must go" and he went and was only allowed back in a subordinate position with a mediocrity on top of him to keep him and his subtleties submerged.

We had a heavenly spring nearly all sunshine and dream. But no doubt your favourites, mist and rain, will assemble to greet you when you land.

I finished "The Avatars, a Futurist Fantasy" and sent it to Macmillan who returned an agreement and sent it to the printers. I have corrected all the galley proofs, and am now

81

expecting page proofs, and can't think of writing anything else until this is out of the way. It follows "The Interpreters" in time. It will be more richly coloured than "The Interpreters" and more of a tale. I don't know what to think of it because I am getting stupid as I get older. I think there are nice things in it and it is packed with pleasant heresies, that is with ancient truths so that it is sure to be denounced by my countrymen. I really do not care. I think it very likely it will be attacked outside Ireland. My fantasy about Avatars is unlike the orthodox conception of an avatar which is a saintly archbishop with the power of working miracles. I say in my book that Avatars are more like divine poets who live out their own lordly imaginations, and that the real traitors in Christianity were not Judas and the priests but the eleven apostles who conspired not to speak about the laughter of Jesus who must have been gay at heart as all immortals were and who went to merrymakings and feasts. You are very good and kind wanting me to go to Glenveagh again. I will collect paints and canvases and stretchers if our tariff system permits of the import of such things. I have painted little and will begin again as an amateur. It will be pleasant indeed to see you again. We can compare pessimistic masterpieces of portraiture of our respective worlds. There is something nice and frank about the German idea that women's business is to breed soldiers and the ideal death is on the battle field. It may be wrong but it is not I think hypocritical. My idea is that women should have no children and that the existing population on earth should pack up their spiritual belong-

ings and get back to Paradise. We have had enough civilisa-
tions. Please give my kind regards to Lucy.

Yours ever
AE

*July 7, Friday.*

[*Written at McKinley's store
at Falcarragh, 1933, on our
way to the island.*]

*Dear AE,*

On arrival we find your letter with the good news you
are coming to-morrow. We have been in England for a
day or so and now are going to Inish Bofin for the night if
my dear old rain doesn't get so bad as to make it impossible. McCann meets you at Letterkenny at 5.35 to-morrow.
Either he will bring you over to Magheraroarty to meet us
or take you to Glenveagh directly as you prefer. The distance for the motor is about the same either way—it is
simply a question of whether you would rather go straight
to Glenveagh and rest until we can get there.

I can't tell you how glad we are you are coming. You
and Donegal are, we feel, the best the world has to offer.

Devotedly,

Kingsley

*41 Sussex Gardens*

*Hyde Park*

*London*

$$\frac{\frac{5}{8}}{33}$$

*Dear Lucy.* I arrived here on Tuesday to find the hottest weather known in London for twenty-two years, and I simply melted and collapsed without energy to write or think about anything and gasped for cool air day and night. . . . I have no news of any kind to tell about myself beyond the heat of London and how difficult it was to leave my friends in Dublin and how bare London seems without them. I swear I will be back in Ireland before a year is up. I think six months of London will give me more than I want to know about it in all my life. Perhaps I think that because most of my friends here are away on holidays. I was to send you a copy of the Avatars but it is not yet published. Macmillan tells me the Book Society has been considering it as their choice of a book for October, and if they select it Macmillan will defer publication until then. I don't suppose they will select it as they must have scores of books more likely to attract their members. But if they did it should mean some more copies distributed than I ever expected. Please give my kind regards to your sisters. I find it difficult to write or think in this heat with perspiration oozing from every pore in my body so that the stupidest detective could track my movements by the perspiration I drop. I do hope dear Lucy, that you have found some

87

peace of mind and that your way of life is now clearer before you. I was so overwhelmed by Kingsley's death that I
was not a very consoling companion for you at such a time.
Time itself is the only healer, and what is the real name of
Time? This is only to let you know that you are much in
my mind.

Yours ever
AE

41 *Sussex Gardens*

*Hyde Park*

*London*

10

10
—
33

*Dear Lucy.* . . . Yes, I was not in the states in the hot summer but I suspect you would have had a heat greater than London in August in your country. And I am sorry for the nation which has to endure it. The heat has faded here to a pleasant chill in the sunny air, and I like it. I have been idling since I came here trying to get some plan of a new book in my mind. I have the ideas, but not the architecture of the book. Anyhow it does not matter much. There are about ten thousand books or more published in the English language every year and one less or more will not matter. I find as I grow older few books are of any real importance to me, only the sacred books and a few with profundities matter to the world in the long run. All the rest are by way of passing the time, and brushing up the normal intelligence a little. I suppose that is worth while. I go on enlarging the circle of acquaintances, trusting to the law of spiritual gravitation to bring to me the folk who belong to me, and it works. Indeed I find too many affinities for comfort or to enable me to have the unbroken leisure for meditation I like. I had a note from Whitehill from Donegal. The sun seems to be miraculously shining there. I gave him an explanation of the rock pictures in caves which was that art at the beginning was regarded as sorcery or black art of some kind and the first poor aesthetes had to hide their art in dark caves lest they might be torn to pieces. But White-hill does not think he could work on that assumption and suggests that I might write about it myself. But I am too wise to make fuller my fantasies except as fantasies and only then when they have some structural significance. But it would make a good primeval tale this, of the savage mad for drawing whose tribe regarded him as a sorcerer and who drew secretly in caves the buffaloes and other creatures whose movements bewitched him. It is the kind of idea I would have chaffed Kingsley about and he would have enjoyed it, might indeed have invented a play around it.

I have no news. The Avatars is just out. I sent you a copy. It is too early, and indeed I no longer have the excitement I had when young over the appearance of a book of mine. One gets almost indifferent about opinions. The only one I know who has read it is Helen Waddell who seemed to like it. I have nothing more to say about myself, except that I am well. I hope you are beginning to get back to average life again. To have the experience you had is like being in a canoe when some rock has slipped into the sea and set the boat rocking furiously in the waves. All waves grow still after a time even the stormiest in our lives, and there is nothing to do but to wait for the subsidence before one can think truly about the experience and be wise about it. Goodby, dear Lucy.

Yours ever

AE.

*41 Sussex Gdns*

*Hyde Park*

*London*

$\dfrac{\begin{array}{r}16\\11\end{array}}{33}$

*Dear Lucy*—The trees in the Park are like this, half blurred in fog and damp, and one's spirits are definitely lower by the effect the external has on the immortal soul. It is humiliating but there it is. I am glad that everything went without causing you more trouble. The thing to do is to get rest for a while, don't fly from things but live the normal life moderately and let the mind be fallow, and come gradually to a normal vision of life. In five or six months you will find your judgment sound and can begin to decide about things. But not before that I suggest.

The papers are a little premature about my movements. My son told me he saw an article in a Chicago paper about my future with an interview with himself which never took place. I have made no decisions. I certainly could not go to U.S.A. while your President is playing pitch and toss with the dollar. If I transferred my small savings into dollars he might playfully depreciate those dollars so that they would not buy me a night's lodging. There is something reassuring about the unexciting slow moving English brain. It is too lazy to think about revolutionary measures and just plods along and its stupidity is often shown to be as wise as the alert wisdom-guided minds of dictators like Roosevelt or Hitler.

I have made a tentative start at a new book but have not really got into it. If I don't I will chuck writing and amuse myself painting for the rest of my days. The Avatars has had some quite good reviews. The Times Literary Supplement was very intelligent. I send you a clipping of it, which may please you as it says pleasant things about a friend.

I have been exploring England a little, was down in Hardy's country, saw the hill where Tess was hung and the blasted tree, and moors as wild as the Irish, and I was down in Sussex in a man-deserted place full of solitude and woods and was pleased by it. I have been meeting interesting folk, the poets De la Mare, Drinkwater, Humbert Wolfe, Sturge Moore, and other folk. But was most interested in a boy of 18 who came to see me, a young mystic and poet who will come to be something fine and good I think. His name is "Sherer", make a note of it and inquire in ten years' time if there is any notability of that name looming up in the world. I have a flair for discovering genius in the young. There is really nothing to write about here. No history is good history. I found last night it was possible in meditation to find a way into the spirit, even in London, the mythic Babylon reincarnated. But then I should have remembered the words of Aratus the Greek poet,

> *"Full of Zeus are the cities, full of Zeus*
> *are the harbours. Full of Zeus are all the*
> *ways of men."*

But one grows to like a place better where one has felt not altogether an exile from the heavenly tribe.

There is nothing more to say now. This is simply a note to say I am alive.

Yours ever<br>A.E.

41 *Sussex Gardens*                                             *16*
*Hyde Park*                                                     $\frac{3}{34}$
*London*

*Dear Lucy.* I got the book from Watkins and duly dec-
orated the first page and gave it back to him. I am writing
this in a hurry as I am making arrangements to leave this
and return to Ireland. I have had enough of London mists
and fogs to satisfy my taste for these things. The people are
nice and kind and one might live pleasurably there. But it
seems they are almost all living a posthumous kind of life.
As if they were once alive in some real world and had
died there and were living on in this the world of the
shades and did not know it. I do not know what my address will be until the 1st of May when it will be c/o Mrs.
Margaret O'Donnell—Parkmore, Ballymore, Co. Donegal.
I have taken a cottage from her for three months, May,
June and July and after that I will try to find some place
in Dublin where I can stay. In Donegal I will try to finish
a book of poetry or get a long way to it. I feel it is a
better atmosphere for my kind of poetry than London, and
I will paint a little in the intervals though as I have no house
to decorate it will be only for the pleasure of painting. But
the Gita says—"Let the motive for action be in the action
itself and not in the event". That is it is right to do things
for the sake of doing them and not for praise or profit or
any such motive. I can do that with painting.

94

Still I am glad I came here for a year as I met many good and new and old friends: Orage, Rothenstein, Stephens, Sturge Moore, Pamela Travers, Ruth Pitter, Helen Waddell and a tribe of poets and such like creatures of my own tribe. I am now arranging the packing of my few pictures and the books I brought over here, and feel a kind of exultation at the thought of being in a country of hills and rocks and sea in a little more than a month. I will be the intervening time in Dublin.

Yours ever

AE.

*c/o Mrs. O'Donnell*
*Parkmore*
*Ballymore*                          *Saturday [July 7, '34]*


*Dear Lucy*

I was on an expedition with my friends who have now
left me, when you came to the Law's. I was sorry but I
had promised to bring them to a place along the coast and
they had little time left. I feel horribly sleepy and tired
with the continual sunlight of the past fortnight and only
hope that when winter comes it will ooze out in some imag-
inative writing. Just now I have not enough imagination to
write a single illuminating sentence. So does the sun drug
its victims. I may go to Dublin in a few days and return
here or rather to a house about fifty feet away, as I find I
have to get clothes and Dublin seems the only place for
such things. If the sun does not stop shining I will soon
be as inert as the rocks. You can tell by the languour of my
sentences how inert I feel already. But if the temperature
lowered I think I would be as active as ever. Heat is the
thing which paralyses me. I was intended for polar circles
but missed my way or could not find a decent family of
Esquimaux to incarnate among and took my chances in
Ireland. O for a large block of ice to sit on and another
lump bound to my forehead and another inside me.

Yours sincerely

AE.

*c/o Mrs. O'Donnell*
*Parkmore*
*Ballymore*                          *Tuesday* [*July 24, '34*]


*Dear Lucy.* I am all at sea and can't make any arrangements
until I hear from a correspondent in London who may be
away on holidays. . . . Macmillan's asked me to write a
volume of reminiscences and I consented and then found I
could not get on with it until I got at my books which are
stored up in London. I can't bring a crate of books here
and I decided I would have to go either to London or
Dublin and get some sort of half permanent rooms there
while I write. I wrote to my old rooms and am expecting to
hear whether they can find room for me at Sussex Gardens
and if they can, when. If they can have me now I will go
over at once. That is why I cannot make any arrangements.
It was kind of you to ask me and Glenveagh is a delightful
place to stay at. But I am moidered about my rooms and
about the book for Macmillan which will take a long time
to write, and I must get at it and break its back before I
get too old to remember anything. I will let you know so
soon as I get a reply from London.

Yours sincerely
AE


97

*1 Brunswick Sq*
*London W. 1*

$$\frac{\begin{array}{c}10\\8\end{array}}{34}$$

*Dear Lucy*

   Your letter has been following me about from Donegal
to Dublin and from Dublin to this place where I have
taken rooms temporarily as I have started a new book and
all my books to which I must refer in writing were stored
up for me in London. I finished a book of verse in Donegal
and I must have some other work to tackle or my mind
will get soft, and so I have made a start at a prose book
which I can work at with some interest. I wanted to stay
longer in Donegal but had to leave at the end of July as the
cottage was engaged for August. I had to come to Dublin
to get clothes and such necessaries and then I found I
could get rooms here and I came yesterday and I think they
will suit me until I can find a permanent address in Dublin.
. . . It must be lovely at Glenveagh now. I see a misty sun
here and imagine what it must be on the lakes and hills in
Donegal. However the sun here does not distract me from
work. Donegal nature does draw me away from the artifice
of writing. I suppose some time you will be in London—
I will see you.

Yours ever

AE.

*14 Tavistock Place*
*Russell Square*
*London W. C. 1*

23
4
35

*Dear Lucy.* Your very kind letter was reforwarded to me here. I would like to be able to say at once "I will come". But I am an invalid. I had intended to take the cottage I had last year in Donegal but had to write saying I did not feel sure I could go. I left Washington breaking off my work there because I had some internal trouble which was making me feel limp as a wet rag, and I dreaded getting laid up in a strange city and returned abruptly to this side of the Atlantic, and consulted a doctor friend who discovered that I had some inflammation in my colon or whatever name is given to the channels through which our foods pass. I was at once put on a pallid diet of barley water, junkett, chicken tea and the like and had to have my insides washed out, and as there are no heat formers in my diet I have to keep warm by artificial means, i.e. sitting beside fires and sleeping with mountains of bed clothes. The drastic treatment is gradually getting my trouble under. But it is a slow business. I had a friend who had the same trouble and it was three months before my friend got over it. You see I cannot get away from proximity to my doctors (I have two) and when I do get over my trouble I know I won't be allowed to eat in the careless way I did all my life, having an admirable digestion, but must live in that way by rule. Now you see

99

why I cannot promise to go anywhere, not at least until I am quite clear from my trouble. You know how I love Donegal yet I had to write to Mrs. Law that I could not take the cottage as I did last year because I did not know whether I would be recovered by the summer. It was very kind of you to invite me to Glenveagh where I had such pleasant holidays. But I am at present unable to say what my movements will be though I long to get out of London, and sit here thinking of the sands and woods and hills around Dunfanaghy. I cannot write for my mind has become as limp as my body. But the treatment is already bringing me a good deal of relief, and I hope by August or September to be well enough to fly from London and be out of the necessity of a regulated diet and attendance by doctors. This is a poor letter to write in answer to an invitation to such a rich beauty as Glenveagh. But it is Karma. I have been healthy all my life and cannot complain if in my age things and forces begin to make me incapable. I may see you if you pass through London. And I envy the lake and hills seeing eyes at Glenveagh.

Yours ever
A.E.

14 Tavistock Place

Russell Sq

London W . C . 1

$$\frac{2}{6}$$

35

*Dear Lucy.* Many thanks for your kind letter. I was not getting any better so a week ago I put myself in the hands of a well-known specialist in this city who gave me a thorough examination, examined me bacteriologically and X-rayed me many times and he has he thinks, located the trouble and hopes in a fortnight that I will be over the worst. But I will have to be careful for the remainder of my life that I do not bring on the same trouble. I have only had two days of his new and drastic treatment so cannot say anything yet about the results but I think already some of the symptoms are subsiding and it was time, for I feel feeble and have grown thin as if I had been starved for weeks and have no energy of mind or body. However if after the fortnight he allows me to move about more and to get a more generous diet I hope I will pick up some of my old vigour. I had hoped to get to Donegal this summer. Now I am not sure whether I will be fit enough to risk being away from my doctors. But I hope I will be out of their hands before summer is over. My case was elucidated to me by the X-ray photographs, and I assume the expert's reading of them is right. Anyhow I am going to follow the treatment with faith as there is no use getting a specialist if one does not carry out his instructions, and I suppose he would not have said that a fortnight would see me over the worst if he did not know. I will write later on if there is any definitive news about myself to impart. After five months of this trouble I hardly feel now energy to take up a pen. But once let me get out of this city into the Irish air and I feel I could recover something at least of my old mental quickness. I have no more now to say except to thank you for your letter and hope to see you sometime when I am recovered.

Yours ever<br>AE

| DATE DUE | | | |
|---|---|---|---|
| | | | |
| | | | |
| | | | |
| | | | |
| | | | |
| | | | |
| | | | |
| | | | |
| | | | |
| | | | |
| | | | |
| | | | |